RISK
IS RIGHT

RISK
IS RIGHT

Better to Lose Your Life Than to Waste It

JOHN PIPER

Foreword by David Platt

CROSSWAY

WHEATON, ILLINOIS

Risk Is Right: Better to Lose Your Life Than to Waste It

Copyright © 2013 by Desiring God Foundation

Published by Crossway
          1300 Crescent Street
          Wheaton, Illinois 60187

First published as "Risk Is Right: Better to Lose Your Life Than to Waste It," chapter 5 in *Don't Waste Your Life* (Crossway), copyright 2003 by Desiring God Foundation, pp. 79–98.

Cover design: Dual Identity, inc.

First printing 2013

Printed in the United States of America

Trade paperback ISBN: 978-1-4335-3534-5
PDF ISBN: 978-1-4335-3535-2
Mobipocket ISBN: 978-1-4335-3536-9
ePub ISBN: 978-1-4335-3537-6

Library of Congress Cataloging-in-Publication Data
Piper, John, 1946-
   Risk is right : better to lose your life than to waste it / John Piper ; foreword by David Platt.
      pages cm
   Includes bibliographical references.
   ISBN 978-1-4335-3534-5 (tp)
1. Christian life. 2. Risk perception. 3. Opportunity. I. Title.
BV4509.5.P567 2013
248.4—dc23   2012043962

Crossway is a publishing ministry of Good News Publishers.

BP   22   21   20   19   18   17   16
15   14   13   12   11   10   9   8   7

CONTENTS

Foreword by David Platt   7

1   The Ultimate Meaning of Life   13

2   What Is Risk?   17

3   Stories of Risk in the Old Testament   23

4   The Great Risk Taker in the New Testament   27

5   When the People of God Risk and When They Don't   33

6   Right and Wrong Reasons to Risk   37

7   The Great Eight and the Foundation of Risk   41

8   On the Far Side of Every Faith-Filled Risk: 47
    Triumphant Love

Desiring God: Note on Resources   53

FOREWORD

David Platt

Retreat or risk? Throughout redemptive history, that question has confronted God's people. As John Piper references in the pages ahead, it was the decision facing the Israelites on a crucial day at Kadesh Barnea. Standing on the brink of the Promised Land, with the guarantee of God within their grasp, they ran from risk and chose to retreat. Instead of staking their lives on the faithfulness of God, they recoiled in fear. The cost was great, and the Lord left an entire generation to waste away in a wilderness until they died.

THE COMMISSION IS CLEAR

Fast-forward a few thousand years, and you come to the people of God standing in a similar moment. We live in a world where half the population is living on less than two dollars a day, and over a billion people dwell in desperate poverty. Such physical need is only surpassed by spiritual poverty. Billions of people are engrossed in the worship of false gods, and approximately two billion of those people are still unreached with the gospel, meaning that they have little chance of even hearing about the sacrifice of Christ for their sins before they die. Most of the unreached live in hard-to-reach areas of the world that are hostile to Christians—areas of the world where our brothers and sisters are presently being persecuted, imprisoned, and killed.

Though the challenges facing the church are great, the commission Christ has given is clear: make disciples of all the nations. Spend your lives spreading the gospel of God for the glory of God to the ends of the earth. As you go, trust in his sovereign authority, depend on his indwelling presence, and experience his incomparable joy.

JESUS IS WORTH IT

As we stand at our Kadesh Barnea, we have a choice. We, too, can retreat into a wilderness of wasted opportunity. We can rest content in casual, convenient, cozy, comfortable Christian lives as we cling to the safety and security this world offers. We can coast through a cultural landscape marked by materialism, characterized by consumerism, and engulfed in individualism. We can assent to the spirit of this age and choose to spend our lives seeking worldly pleasures, acquiring worldly possessions, and pursuing worldly ambitions—all under the banner of cultural Christianity.

Or we can decide that Jesus is worth more than this. We can recognize that he has created us, saved us, and called us for a much greater purpose than anything this world could ever offer us. We can die to ourselves, our hopes, our dreams, our ambitions, our priorities, and our plans. We can do all of this because we believe that the person and the plan of Christ bring reward that makes any risk more than worth it.

POWERED BY GOSPEL JOY

In Matthew 13:44 Jesus tells his disciples, "The kingdom of heaven is like treasure hidden in a field, which a man found and covered up. Then in his joy he goes and sells all that he has and buys that field."

I love this picture. Imagine walking in a field and stumbling upon a treasure that is more valuable than anything else you could work for or find in this life. It is more valuable than all you have now or will ever have in the future. You look around and notice that no one else realizes the treasure is here, so you cover it up quickly and walk away, pretending you haven't seen anything. You go into town and begin to sell off all your possessions to have enough money to buy that field. The world thinks you're crazy.

"What are you thinking?" your friends and family ask you.

You tell them, "I'm buying that field over there."

They look at you in disbelief. "That's foolish," they say. "Why are you giving away everything you have to buy that field?"

You respond, "I have a hunch," and you smile to yourself

as you walk away. You smile because you know that in the end any risk that others perceive is nothing compared to the reward you will receive. So with joy—with joy!—you sell it all. Why? Because you have found something worth losing everything else for.

This is the picture of Jesus in the gospel. He is something—someone—worth losing everything for. When we really believe this, then risking everything we are and everything we have, to know and obey Christ is no longer a matter of sacrifice. It's just common sense. To let go of the pursuits, possessions, pleasures, safety, and security of this world in order to follow Jesus wherever he leads, no matter what it costs, is not sacrificial as much as it is smart. In the words of Jim Elliot, "He is no fool who gives what he cannot keep to gain what he cannot lose."

FEARLESS IN THE FACE OF RISK

I praise God for John Piper and the way he has shown me and countless others the supremacy of Christ. I was in college when I heard my first Piper sermon, entitled "Christ Died for God." I was compelled by a captivating, biblical vision of a God-centered God, and I began to realize in a fresh way that the ultimate reason for my existence is God's exaltation. Moreover, I began to recognize that my greatest joy is indeed found in God's greatest glory, and Christ is clearly a treasure worth losing and letting go of everything for. This is a central theme (maybe *the* central theme) of Scripture and is the predominant truth that pervades John Piper's ministry, which is why this book by him on risk makes so much sense.

I pray that God will use it, along with a host of other things, to raise up an army of pastors, missionaries, church leaders, and church members who are fearless in the face of risk because they realize that in Christ, even death is reward. In view of God's great glory above us and in light of the world's great need around us, retreat is unquestionably wrong. For the good of our souls and for the glory of our Savior, risk is most assuredly right.

Chapter One

THE ULTIMATE MEANING OF LIFE

Almost everything I have to say is summed up in Paul's passionate words to the church in Philippi:

> It is my eager expectation and hope that I will not be at all ashamed, but that with full courage now as always Christ will be honored in my body, whether by life or by death. For to me to live is Christ, and to die is gain. (Phil. 1:20–21)

If you had asked Paul to tell you what the ultimate aim of life is—*his* life or *any* unwasted life—I think this is what he would have said. Honoring Christ, magnifying Christ, making much of Christ. That was the meaning of Paul's life. It should be the meaning of ours. And Paul prays it will be the meaning of his death as well. We live and we die to make much of Christ.

The universe was created for this—making much of Christ. Paul says as much in Colossians 1:16: "All things were created through him and *for* him." *For* him. That is, for his glory. For his admiration, esteem, wonder, praise, trust, obedience, allegiance, worship. This meaning of life is global. It embraces all the peoples of the world. Why did God call Paul and make him—and thousands after him—an emissary of the gospel to the nations? He answers, "We have received grace and apostleship to bring about the obedience of faith *for the sake of his name* among all the nations" (Rom. 1:5). For the sake of Jesus's name.

After Jesus had died and made an atonement for sins, God raised him from the dead and "highly exalted him and bestowed on him the name that is above every name" (Phil. 2:9). The reason God did this was the universal acclaim of Jesus Christ. He raised him "so that *at the name of Jesus* every knee should bow, in heaven and on earth and under the earth" (Phil. 2:10). John Stott warns against the treasonous imperialisms of using world missions as a cloak for pursuing honor for our own nation or church or organization, or ourselves. Then he says stunningly: "Only one imperialism is Christian, however, and that is concern for His Imperial Majesty Jesus Christ, and for the glory of his empire or kingdom."[1]

This is what we live for, and die for: to make much of Jesus Christ and his glorious, universe-encompassing kingdom. The heart cry of our lives, young and old, men and women, rich and poor, is the glory of Jesus Christ so that *with full courage*

---

[1] John Stott, *The Message of Romans* (Downers Grove, IL: InterVarsity, 1994), 53.

now as always Christ might be honored in our bodies, whether by life or by death.

There are a thousand ways to magnify Christ in life and death. None should be scorned. All are important. But none makes the worth of Christ shine more brightly than sacrificial love for other people in the name of Jesus. If Christ is so valuable that the hope of his immediate and eternal fellowship after death frees us from the self-serving fear of dying and enables us to lay down our lives for the good of others, such love magnifies the glory of Christ like nothing else in the world.

The Bible tells us that Jesus endured the cross "for the joy that was set before him" (Heb. 12:2)—the joy of being raised from the dead, returning to the glory of the Father, saving innumerable people from destruction, making the whole universe new, and being surrounded by countless worshipers forever. There never has been a greater act of love than that Jesus laid down his life to save sinners (John 15:13; Rom. 5:6-8). Therefore, the greatest act of love was enabled by hope of joy beyond the grave.

If Jesus was carried through the hour of death for the sake of others by hope of joy in the presence of God, we would be arrogant to presume we could be carried through death for others without such hope. The early Christians gave their property and their lives for sake of others because they knew that on the other side of death Jesus would be their great reward. "You had compassion on those in prison, and you joyfully accepted the plundering of your property, *since you knew that you yourselves had a better possession and an abiding one*" (Heb. 10:34).

Now we are ready to talk about risk.

Chapter Two

WHAT IS RISK?

If our single, all-embracing passion is to make much of Christ in life and death, and if the life that magnifies him most is the life of costly love, then life is risk, and risk is right. To run from it is to waste your life.

WHAT IS RISK?

I define risk very simply as an action that exposes you to the possibility of loss or injury. If you take a risk you can lose money, you can lose face, you can lose your health or even your life. And what's worse, if you take a risk, you may endanger other people and not just yourself. Their lives may be at stake also. Will a wise and loving person, then, ever take a risk? Is it wise to expose yourself to loss? Is it loving to endanger others? Is losing life the same as wasting it?

It depends. Of course you can throw your life away in a hundred sinful ways and die as a result. In that case, losing life and wasting it would be the same. But losing life is not always the same as wasting it. What if the circumstances are such that *not* taking a risk will result in loss and injury? It may not be wise to play it safe. And what if a successful risk would bring great benefit to many people, and its failure would bring harm only to yourself? It may not be loving to choose comfort or security when something great may be achieved for the cause of Christ and for the good of others.

RISK IS WOVEN INTO THE FABRIC OF OUR FINITE LIVES

Why is there such a thing as risk? Because there is such a thing as ignorance. If there were no ignorance about the future, there would be no risk. Risk is possible because we don't know how things will turn out. This means that God can take no risks.[1] He knows the outcome of all his choices before they happen. This is what it means to be God over against all the gods of the nations (Isa. 41:23; 42:8–9; 44:6–8; 45:21; 46:8–11; 48:3). And since he knows the outcome of all his actions before they happen, he plans accordingly. His omniscience rules out the very possibility of taking risks.[2]

But not so with us. We are not God; we are ignorant. We

---

[1] This view is clearly and consciously opposed to the view called "open theism," which believes that God takes real risks in the sense that he does not know the outcome of many events that he sets in motion. This view is represented, for example, by John Sanders, *The God Who Risks: A Theology of Providence* (Downers Grove, IL: InterVarsity, 1998); and Gregory A. Boyd, *Satan and the Problem of Evil: Constructing a Trinitarian Warfare Theodicy* (Downers Grove, IL: InterVarsity, 2001), and is criticized effectively, I believe, by R. K. McGregor Wright, *No Place for Sovereignty: What's Wrong with Freewill Theism?* (Downers Grove, IL: InterVarsity, 1996); Bruce A. Ware, *God's Lesser Glory: The Diminished God of Open Theism* (Wheaton, IL: Crossway, 2000); John M. Frame, *No Other God: A Response to Open Theism* (Phillipsburg, NJ: P&R, 2001); and John Piper, Justin Taylor, Paul Kjoss Helseth, eds., *Beyond the Bounds: Open Theism and the Undermining of Biblical Christianity* (Wheaton, IL: Crossway, 2003).

[2] See more on why God cannot be a risk taker in John Piper, *The Pleasures of God: Meditations on God's Delight in Being God*, 3rd ed. (Colorado Springs: Multnomah, 2012), 40–46.

don't know what will happen tomorrow. God does not tell us in detail what he intends to do tomorrow or five years from now. Evidently God intends for us to live and act in ignorance and in uncertainty about many of the outcomes of our actions.

He says to us, for example, in James 4:13–15:

> Come now, you who say, "Today or tomorrow we will go into such and such a town and spend a year there and trade and make a profit"—yet you do not know what tomorrow will bring. What is your life? For you are a mist that appears for a little time and then vanishes. Instead you ought to say, "If the Lord wills, we will live and do this or that."

You don't know if your heart will stop before you finish reading this page. You don't know if some oncoming driver will swerve out of his lane and hit you head-on in the next week. You don't know if the food in the restaurant may have some deadly bacteria in it. You don't know if a stroke may paralyze you before the week is out, or if some man with a rifle will shoot you at the shopping center. We are not God. We do not know about tomorrow.

EXPLODING THE MYTH OF SAFETY

Therefore, risk is woven into the fabric of our finite lives. We cannot avoid risk even if we want to. Ignorance and uncertainty about tomorrow is our native air. All of our plans for tomorrow's activities can be shattered by a thousand unknowns whether we stay at home under the covers or ride the freeways. One of my aims is to explode the myth of safety and to somehow deliver you from the enchantment of security. Because it's a mirage. It doesn't exist. Every direction you turn, there are unknowns and things beyond your control.

The futility of finding a risk-free place to stand has paralyzed many of us. I have tasted this in my own pastoral leadership. There are decisions to be made, but I can't see which decision is best. There are so many unknowns. The temptation is to run away—if not physically, emotionally. Just think about something else. Put it off. Procrastinate. Hope the problem goes away. But it doesn't. And our paralysis is serving no one. The paralyzing fear of making a decision serves no one. It is cowardly. Risk is the only way forward.

BONHOEFFER ON THE LOVELESSNESS OF INDECISION

Dietrich Bonhoeffer breathed the air of crisis most of his adult life. This would eventually make the issue of decisiveness a matter of life and death. And even before that moment it was an issue of love.

Everywhere Bonhoeffer looked in the Europe of 1934 he saw Christian indecisiveness. The "deutsche Christen," the global ecumenical movement—everyone but Hitler. Nazism's stranglehold on the church in Germany was almost complete, and no one seemed willing to act.

Bonhoeffer and his friends soon would. A "confessing church" would emerge, struggling to be free from coercions of the Third Reich. A "Barmen Declaration" would be published. But for now Bonhoeffer pleaded for action.

On April 7, 1934, he wrote a letter to Henry Louis Henriod, the Swiss theologian who headed the ecumenical World Alliance. He pled for support for the pastors and Christians in Germany who knew (to their peril) their church was no longer a church. Here we learn a lesson about the perils of indecision. Bonhoeffer wrote:

> A decision must be made at some point, and it's no good waiting indefinitely for a sign from heaven that will solve the difficulty without further trouble. Even the ecumenical movement has to make up its mind and is therefore subject to error, like everything human. But to procrastinate and prevaricate simply because you're afraid of erring, when others—I mean our brethren in Germany—must make infinitely more difficult decisions every day, seems to me almost to run counter to love. *To delay or fail to make decisions may be more sinful than to make wrong decisions out of faith and love.*[3]

That last sentence is worth a long consideration. Risk avoidance may be more sinful—more unloving—than taking the risk in faith and love and making a wrong decision. In my

---

[3] Eric Metaxas, *Bonhoeffer: Pastor, Martyr, Prophet, Spy* (Nashville: Nelson, 2010), 218; emphasis added.

ministry, I have often said after making a hard decision where both directions are painful, "This is why I love the gospel." Doing nothing needs forgiveness as much as doing the best you can and erring.

There is sometimes a subtle selfishness behind our avoidance of risk taking. There is a hypocrisy that lets us take risks every day for *ourselves* but paralyzes us from taking risks for *others* on the Calvary road of love. We are deluded and think that such risk may jeopardize a security that in fact does not even exist. The way I hope to explode the myth of safety and to disenchant you with the mirage of security is simply to go to the Bible and show that it is right to risk for the cause of Christ. It is right to seek to make much of Christ by taking the risks of love.

Chapter Three

STORIES OF RISK IN THE OLD TESTAMENT

It is amazing that the apostle Paul would say something so sweeping about the whole Old Testament—and I assume that it is all the more true of the New Testament. He said, "Whatever was written in former days was written for our instruction, that through endurance and through the encouragement of the Scriptures we might have hope" (Rom. 15:4). All the historical stories, all the laws, all the proverbs and psalms, all the prophecies—"*whatever* was written"—was meant to give us *hope.*

And hope is the great power to love people in the face of serious danger. God-given hope creates the power to risk for the sake of others. Paul spoke to the Colossians of "the love that you have for all the saints, because of the hope laid up for you in heaven" (Col. 1:5). Love *because of* hope. So for the sake of love, let's look at some of "what was written for our hope"—some of the great stories of risk in the Old Testament.

"MAY THE LORD DO WHAT SEEMS GOOD TO HIM"

Let's start with 2 Samuel 10. The Amalekites had shamed the messengers of Israel and made themselves odious in the sight of David. To protect themselves they had hired the Syrians to fight with them against the Israelites. Joab, the commander of Israel's forces, found himself surrounded with Amalekites on one side and Syrians on the other. So he divided his troops, put his brother Abishai in charge of one troop of fighters, and led the other himself.

In verse 11 they pledged to help each other. Then comes this great word in verse 12: "Be of good courage, and let us be courageous for our people, and for the cities of our God, and may the LORD do what seems good to him." What do these last words mean, "May the LORD do what seems good to him"? They mean that Joab had made a strategic decision for the cities of God, and he did not know how it would turn out. He had no special revelation from God on this issue. He had to make a decision on the basis of sanctified wisdom. He had to risk or run. He did not know how it would turn out. So he made his decision, and he handed the results over to God. And this was right.

"IF I PERISH, I PERISH"

Queen Esther is another example of courageous risk in the service of love and for the glory of God. There was a Jewish man named Mordecai who lived in the fifth century before

Christ during the Jews' exile. He had a younger orphaned cousin named Esther whom he had adopted as a daughter. She grew up to be beautiful and eventually was taken by Persia's King Ahasuerus to be his queen. Haman, one of Ahasuerus's chief princes, hated Mordecai and all the Jewish refugees and persuaded the king to decree that they be exterminated. The king did not realize that his own queen was a Jew.

Mordecai sent word to Esther to go before the king and plead the case of her people. But Esther knew there was a royal law that anyone who approached the king without being called would be put to death, unless he lifted his golden scepter. She also knew that her people's lives were at stake. Esther sent her response to Mordecai with these words:

> Go, gather all the Jews to be found in Susa, and hold a fast on my behalf, and do not eat or drink for three days, night or day. I and my young women will also fast as you do. Then I will go to the king, though it is against the law, and if I perish, I perish. (Est. 4:15–16)

"If I perish, I perish." What does that mean? It means that Esther did not know what the outcome of her act would be. She had no special revelation from God. She made her decision on the basis of wisdom and love for her people and trust in God. She had to risk or run. She did not know how it would turn out. So she made her decision and handed the results over to God. "If I perish, I perish." And this was right.

"WE WILL NOT SERVE YOUR GODS"

Consider one more example from the Old Testament. The setting is Babylon. The Jewish people are in exile. The king is Nebuchadnezzar. He sets up an image of gold, then commands that when the trumpet sounds, all the people will bow down to the image. But Shadrach, Meshach, and Abednego did not bow down. They worshiped the one true God of Israel.

So Nebuchadnezzar threatened them and said that if they did not worship the image, they would be thrown into the fiery furnace. They answered:

> O Nebuchadnezzar, we have no need to answer you in this matter. If this be so, our God whom we serve is able to deliver us from the burning fiery furnace, and he will deliver us out of your hand, O king. But if not, be it known to you, O king, that we will not serve your gods or worship the golden image that you have set up. (Dan. 3:16–18)

This was sheer risk. "We believe our God will deliver us. But even if he doesn't, we will not serve your gods." They did not know how it would turn out. They said virtually the same thing Esther said: "If we perish, we perish." And they handed the outcome to God the same way Joab and Abishai did: "And may the Lord do what seems good to him." And this was right. It is right to risk for the cause of God.

Chapter Four

THE GREAT RISK TAKER IN THE NEW TESTAMENT

The great New Testament risk taker was the apostle Paul. Picture him first on his way to Jerusalem after years of suffering for Christ almost everywhere he went. He had bound himself in the Holy Spirit (Acts 19:21) to go to Jerusalem. He had collected money for the poor, and he was going to see that it was delivered faithfully. He got as far as Caesarea, and a prophet named Agabus came down from Judea, symbolically bound his own hands and feet with Paul's belt, and said, "Thus says the Holy Spirit, 'This is how the Jews at Jerusalem will bind the man who owns this belt and deliver him into the hands of the Gentiles'" (Acts 21:11).

"I AM READY TO DIE FOR THE NAME OF THE LORD JESUS"

When the believers heard this, they begged Paul not to go to Jerusalem. He responded, "What are you doing, weeping and breaking my heart? For I am ready not only to be imprisoned but even to die in Jerusalem for the name of the Lord Jesus"

(Acts 21:13). Then, Luke tells us, his friends relented: "And since he would not be persuaded, we ceased and said, 'Let the will of the Lord be done'" (Acts 21:14).

In other words, Paul believed that this trip to Jerusalem was necessary for the cause of Christ. He did not know the details of what would happen there or what the outcome would be. Arrest and affliction for sure. But then what? Death? Imprisonment? Banishment? No one knew. So what did they say? They could agree on one thing: "The will of the Lord be done!" Or as Joab said, "May the LORD do what seems good to him." And this was right.

"IN EVERY CITY . . . AFFLICTIONS AWAIT ME"

In fact, Paul's whole life was one stressful risk after another. He said in Acts 20:23, "The Holy Spirit testifies to me in every city that imprisonment and afflictions await me." But he never knew in what form they would come, or when they would come, or by whom they would come. Paul had decided to risk his life in Jerusalem with the full knowledge of what it might be like. What he had already endured left him no doubt about what might happen in Jerusalem:

> Five times I received at the hands of the Jews the forty lashes less one. Three times I was beaten with rods. Once I was stoned. Three times I was shipwrecked; a night and a day I was adrift at sea; on frequent journeys, in danger from

rivers, danger from robbers, danger from my own people, danger from Gentiles, danger in the city, danger in the wilderness, danger at sea, danger from false brothers; in toil and hardship, through many a sleepless night, in hunger and thirst, often without food, in cold and exposure. And, apart from other things, there is the daily pressure on me of my anxiety for all the churches. (2 Cor. 11:24–28)

What does this mean? It means that Paul never knew where the next blow would come from. Every day he risked his life for the cause of God. The roads weren't safe. The rivers weren't safe. His own people, the Jews, weren't safe. The Gentiles weren't safe. The cities weren't safe. The wilderness wasn't safe. The sea wasn't safe. Even the so-called Christian brothers weren't safe. Safety was a mirage. It didn't exist for the apostle Paul.

He had two choices: waste his life or live with risk. And he answered this choice clearly: "But I do not account my life of any value nor as precious to myself, if only I may finish my course and the ministry that I received from the Lord Jesus, to testify to the gospel of the grace of God" (Acts 20:24). He never knew what the day would hold. But the Calvary road beckoned. And he risked his life every day. And this was right.

"IF THEY PERSECUTED ME, THEY WILL ALSO PERSECUTE YOU"

Lest we think that this risk-taking life was unique to Paul, he made it a point to tell young Christians that they would meet unspecified troubles. After establishing new churches on his first missionary journey, he returned some months later "strengthening the souls of the disciples, encouraging them to continue in the faith, and saying that *through many tribulations we must enter the kingdom of God*" (Acts 14:22). When he wrote to the young Thessalonian church, he expressed concern that they might have been shaken by their afflictions and said to them, "You yourselves know that we have been destined for this [that is, for these afflictions]" (1 Thess. 3:3). In other words, the Christian life is a call to risk.

Jesus had made this clear. He said, for example, in Luke 21:16, "You will be delivered up even by parents and brothers and relatives and friends, and some of you they will put to death." The key word here is *some*. "Some of you they will put to death." This word puts the earthly life of the disciples in great uncertainty. Not all will die for the cause of Christ. But not all will live either. Some will die. And some will live. This is what I mean by risk. It is the will of God that we be uncertain about how life on this earth will turn out for us. And therefore it is the will of the Lord that we take risks for the cause of God.

Life was hard for Jesus, and he said it would be hard for his followers. "Remember the word that I said to you: 'A servant is not greater than his master.' If they persecuted me, they will also persecute you" (John 15:20). So Peter warned the churches of Asia that mistreatment would be normal. "Beloved, do not be surprised at the fiery trial when it comes upon you to test you, as though something strange were happening to you. But rejoice insofar as you share Christ's sufferings, that you may also rejoice and be glad when his glory is revealed. If you are insulted for the name of Christ, you are blessed, because the Spirit of glory and of God rests upon you" (1 Pet. 4:12–14).

Chapter Five

WHEN THE PEOPLE OF GOD RISK AND WHEN THEY DON'T

The first three centuries of the Christian church set the pattern of growth under threat. Stephen Neill, in his *History of Christian Missions*, wrote, "Undoubtedly, Christians under the Roman Empire had no legal right to existence, and were liable to the utmost stringency of the law. . . . Every Christian knew that sooner or later he might have to testify to his faith at the cost of his life."[1]

Might. There's the risk. It was always there. Maybe we will be killed for being Christians. Maybe we won't. It is a risk. That was normal. And to become a Christian under those circumstances was right.

THE GENERATIONS WHO RISKED

In fact, it was the Christ-exalting love that the Christians showed in spite of risk that stunned the pagan world. The Roman emperor Julian (AD 332–363) wanted to breathe new life into the

[1] Stephen Neill, *A History of Christian Missions* (Middlesex, UK: Penguin, 1964), 42–43.

ancient pagan religion but saw more and more people drawn to Christianity. He wrote with frustration against these "atheists" (who did not believe in the Roman gods, but in Christ):

> Atheism [i.e., Christian faith] has been specially advanced through the loving service rendered to strangers, and through their care for the burial of the dead. It is a scandal there is not a single Jew who is a beggar, and that the god-less Galileans care not only for their own poor but for ours as well; while those who belong to us look in vain for the help that we should render them.[2]

It is costly to follow Christ. There is risk everywhere. But this very risk is the means by which the value of Christ shines more brightly.

THE GENERATION THAT DID NOT RISK

But what happens when the people of God do not escape from the beguiling enchantment of security? What happens if they try to live their lives in the mirage of safety? The answer is wasted lives. Do you remember the time it happened?

It had been less than three years since the people of Israel came out of Egypt by the power of God. Now they were on the borders of the Promised Land. The Lord said to Moses, "Send men to spy out the land of Canaan, which I am giving to the people of Israel" (Num. 13:2). So Moses sent Caleb, Joshua,

---

[2] Ibid., 42.

and ten other men. After forty days they returned with a huge cluster of grapes hung on a pole between two men. Caleb issued the hope-filled call to his people: "Let us go up at once and occupy it, for we are well able to overcome it" (Num. 13:30). But the others said, "We are not able to go up against the people, for they are stronger than we are" (v. 31).

Caleb was unable to explode the myth of safety. The people were gripped by the beguiling enchantment of security—the notion that there is a sheltered way of life apart from the path of God-exalting obedience. They murmured against Moses and Aaron and decided to go back to Egypt—the great mirage of safety. Joshua tried to free them from their stupor.

> The land, which we passed through to spy it out, is an exceedingly good land. If the LORD delights in us, he will bring us into this land and give it to us, a land that flows with milk and honey. Only do not rebel against the LORD. And do not fear the people of the land, for they are bread for us. Their protection is removed from them, and the LORD is with us; do not fear them. (Num. 14:7–9)

But not even Joshua could explode the myth of safety. The people were drunk in a dream world of security. And they tried to stone Caleb and Joshua. The result was thousands of wasted lives and wasted years. It was clearly wrong not to take the risk of battling the giants in the land of Canaan. Oh, how much is wasted when we do not risk for the cause of God!

Chapter Six

RIGHT AND WRONG REASONS TO RISK

Risk is right. And the reason is not that God promises success to all our ventures in his cause. There is no promise that every effort for the cause of God will succced, at least not in the short run.

SHORT-TERM SUCCESS NOT PROMISED

When King Herod divorced his wife in order to take his brother's wife, John the Baptist risked calling him an adulterer. For this John got his head chopped off. And he had done right to risk his life for the cause of God and truth. Jesus had no criticism for him, but only the highest praise (Matt. 11:11).

Paul risked going up to Jerusalem to complete his ministry to the poor. He was beaten and thrown in prison for two years and then shipped off to Rome and executed there two years later. And he did right to risk his life for the cause of Christ. How many graves are there in Africa and Asia because thousands of young missionaries were freed by the power of the Holy Spirit from the enchantment of security and then risked their lives to make much of Christ among the unreached peoples of the world!

And now what about you? Are you caught in the enchantment of security, paralyzed from taking any risks for the cause of God? Or have you been freed by the power of the Holy Spirit from the mirage of Egyptian safety and comfort? Do you men ever say with Joab, "For the sake of the name, I'll try it! And may the Lord do what seems good to him"? Do you women ever say with Esther, "For the sake of Christ, I'll try it! And if I perish, I perish"?

RISKING FOR THE WRONG REASONS

There is more than one danger in calling Christians to take risks. For one, we might become so fixated on self-denial that we are unable to enjoy the proper pleasures of this life that God has given for our good. Another danger, which is worse, is that we might be drawn to a life of risk for self-exalting reasons. We might feel the adrenaline of heroism rising. We might scorn the lazy and cowardly and feel superior. We might think of risk as a kind of righteousness that makes us acceptable to God. What would be missing from all these mistakes is childlike faith in the sovereign rule of God and in his triumphant love.

I have been assuming that the power and the motive behind taking risks for the cause of God is not heroism, or the lust for adventure, or the courage of self-reliance, or the need to earn God's good will, but rather faith in the all-providing, all-ruling, all-satisfying Son of God, Jesus Christ. The strength to risk losing face for the sake of Christ is the faith that God's love will lift up your face in the end and vindicate your cause. The strength to risk losing money for the cause of the gospel is the faith that we have a treasure in the heavens that cannot fail. The strength to risk losing life in this world is faith in the promise that he who loses his life in this world will save it for the age to come.

This is very different from heroism and self-reliance. When we risk losing face or money or life because we believe God will always help us and use our loss, in the end, to make us more glad in his glory, then it's not we who get the praise because of our courage; it's God who gets the praise because of his care. In this way risk reflects God's value, not our valor.

This foundation for fearlessness must not be assumed. We are wired to risk for the wrong reasons. Without Christ, we are all legalists or lechers at heart—wanting to do our own thing, or wanting to do God's thing in our way to prove our own ability. Since we are wired this way, we need protection. God has given us another way to pursue risk. Do it "by the strength that God supplies—in order that in everything

God may be glorified through Jesus Christ" (1 Pet. 4:11). And the way God supplies his strength is through faith in his promises. Every loss we risk, in order to make much of Christ, God promises to restore a thousandfold with his all-satisfying fellowship.

Chapter Seven

THE GREAT EIGHT AND THE FOUNDATION OF RISK

Earlier I mentioned Luke 21:16, where Jesus says to his disciples, "Some of you they will put to death." But I did not mention the promise that follows: "You will be hated by all for my name's sake. *But not a hair of your head will perish*" (v. 18). This is one of those painful paradoxes in the Bible: "Some of you they will put to death. . . . But not a hair of your head will perish"! What does this mean? What is Jesus trying to say to us when he says, "Go ahead and risk obedience; some of you they will put to death; but not a hair of your head will perish"?

THE GREAT EIGHT

I think the best commentary on these verses in Luke 21 is Romans 8:35–39. Romans 8 is sometimes called "The Great Eight" because the heights of our salvation and the depths of its foundation are concentrated here in a way that is greater than anywhere else in the Bible. There is no better description of how deep the sure foundations are of the hope that frees us to risk everything for Jesus.

> Who shall separate us from the love of Christ? Shall tribulation, or distress, or persecution, or famine, or nakedness, or danger, or sword? As it is written, "For your sake we are being killed all the day long; we are regarded as sheep to be slaughtered." No, in all these things we are more than conquerors through him who loved us. For I am sure that neither death nor life, nor angels nor rulers, nor things present nor things to come, nor powers, nor height nor depth, nor anything else in all creation, will be able to separate us from the love of God in Christ Jesus our Lord.

Compare these terrible and wonderful words with what Jesus said: "Some of you they will put to death. . . . But not a hair of your head will perish." Like Jesus, Paul says that the love of Christ for us does not eliminate our suffering. On the contrary, our very attachment to Christ will bring suffering. What is Paul's answer to his own question in verse 35: "Shall tribulation, or distress, or persecution, or famine, or nakedness, or danger, or sword separate us from the love of Christ?"

His answer in verse 37 is a resounding *No!* But don't miss the implication of the question: The reason these things will not separate us from the love of Christ is not that they don't happen to people whom Christ loves. They do. Paul's quoting of Psalm 44:22 shows that these things do in fact happen to Christ's people. "For your sake we are being killed all the day long; we are regarded as sheep to be slaughtered." In other words, Christ's love for us does not spare us these sufferings. Risk is real. The Christian life is a painful life. Not joyless. But not painless either.

DOES GOD REALLY SUPPLY ALL WE NEED?

This is the meaning of the little word "in" found in verse 37: "*In* all these things we are more than conquerors . . ." We are more than conquerors *in* our afflictions, not by avoiding them. So Paul agrees with Jesus: "Some of you they will put to death." Obedience is risk. And it is right to risk for the cause of God. Some of the risks are mentioned in verse 35:

- "tribulation"—the trouble and oppression of various kinds that Paul says we must walk through on our way to heaven (Acts 14:22).
- "distress"—calamities that bring stress and threaten to break us like a stick (2 Cor. 6:4; 12:10).
- "persecution"—active opposition from the enemies of the gospel (Matt. 5:11–12).
- "danger"—every kind of threat or menace to body, soul, and family (2 Cor. 11:26).
- "sword"—the weapon that killed James (Acts 12:2).
- "famine and nakedness"—the lack of food and clothing.

I put "famine and nakedness" last because they pose the greatest problem. Did not Jesus say:

> Do not be anxious about your life, what you will eat or what you will drink, nor about your body, what you will put on. Is not life more than food, and the body more than clothing? . . . Do not be anxious, saying, "What shall we eat?" or "What shall we drink?" or "What shall we wear?". . . Your heavenly Father knows that you need them all. But seek first the kingdom of God and his righteousness, and all these things will be added to you. (Matt. 6:25, 31–33)

"Well, which is it?" we might ask. Are Christians subject to "famine and nakedness," or will God provide "all these things" when we need them? Will Christians never hunger or starve or be ill-clothed? Have not some of the greatest saints in the world been stripped and starved?

What about Hebrews 11:37–38? "They were stoned, they were sawn in two, they were killed with the sword. They went about in skins of sheep and goats, destitute, afflicted, mistreated—of whom the world was not worthy—wandering about in deserts and mountains, and in dens and caves of the earth." The losses and miseries of these believers was not owing to their unbelief. They were faithful—people "of whom the world was not worthy."

ALL YOU NEED TO DO HIS WILL AND BE HAPPY FOREVER

What, then, does Jesus mean, "All these things—all your food and clothing—will be added to you when you seek the kingdom of God first"? He means the same thing he meant when he said, "Some of you they will put to death. . . . But not a hair of your head will perish" (Luke 21:16–18). He meant that you will have everything you need to do his will and be eternally and supremely happy in him.

How much food and clothing are necessary? Necessary for what? we must ask. Necessary to be comfortable? No, Jesus did not promise comfort. Necessary to avoid shame? No, Jesus called us to bear shame for his name with joy. Necessary to stay alive? No, he did not promise to spare us death—of any kind. Persecution and plague consume the saints. Christians die on the scaffold, and Christians die of disease. That's why Paul wrote, "We ourselves, who have the firstfruits of the Spirit, groan inwardly as we wait eagerly for adoption as sons, the redemption of our bodies" (Rom. 8:23).

What Jesus meant was that our Father in heaven would never let us be tested beyond what we are able (1 Cor. 10:13). If there is one scrap of bread that you need, as God's child, in order to maintain your faith in the dungeon of starvation, you will have it. God does not promise enough food for comfort or life—he promises enough so that you can trust him and do his will.[1]

---

[1] This is the way I would understand the many general promises in the Old Testament to the effect that the needs of the righteous will always be met. For example, Proverbs 10:3, "The Lord does not let the righteous go hungry, but he thwarts the craving of the wicked." I think this is (1) generally true in the way God runs the world—upright, hardworking people prosper and have enough; and (2) always and absolutely true in the sense that the righteous will never hun-

I CAN DO ALL THINGS THROUGH CHRIST—EVEN STARVE

When Paul promised, "My God will supply every need of yours according to his riches in glory in Christ Jesus," he had just said, "I know how to be brought low, and I know how to abound. In any and every circumstance, I have learned the secret of facing plenty and *hunger*, abundance and *need*. I can do all things through him who strengthens me" (Phil. 4:12–13, 19). "All things" means "I can suffer hunger through him who strengthens me. I can be destitute of food and clothing through him who strengthens me." That is what Jesus promises. He will never leave us or forsake us (Heb. 13:5). If we starve, he will be our everlasting, life-giving bread. If we are shamed with nakedness, he will be our perfect, all-righteous apparel. If we are tortured and made to scream in our dying pain, he will keep us from cursing his name and will restore our beaten body to everlasting beauty.

---

ger beyond what they are able to endure for the sake of Christ. See John Piper, "'No Evil Will Befall You.' Really? Beware of Satan's Use of Psalms" in *Taste and See: Savoring the Supremacy of God in All of Life* (Sisters, OR: Multnomah, 2005), 46–48.

Chapter Eight

ON THE FAR SIDE OF EVERY FAITH-FILLED RISK: TRIUMPHANT LOVE

The bottom-line comfort and assurance in all our risk taking for Christ is that nothing will ever separate us from the love of Christ. Paul asks, "Shall tribulation, or distress, or persecution, or famine, or nakedness, or danger, or sword *separate us from the love of Christ*?" (Rom. 8:35). His answer is *No!* In other words, no misery that a true Christian ever experiences is evidence that he has been cut off from the love of Christ. The love of Christ triumphs over all misery. Romans 8:38–39 makes this crystal-clear: "For I am sure that neither death nor life, nor angels nor rulers, nor things present nor things to come, nor powers, nor height nor depth, nor anything else in all creation, will be able to separate us from the love of God in Christ Jesus our Lord."

On the far side of every risk—even if it results in death— the love of God triumphs. This is the faith that frees us to risk for the cause of God. It is not heroism, or lust for adventure, or courageous self-reliance, or efforts to earn God's favor. It is childlike faith in the triumph of God's love—that on the other side of all our risks, for the sake of righteousness, God will still be holding us. We will be eternally satisfied in him. Nothing will have been wasted.

HOW CAN IT GET BETTER THAN BEING CONQUERORS?

But there is even more to the promise that sustains us in times of risk for Christ's sake. Paul asks, "If God is for us, who can be against us?" (Rom. 8:31). The answer he intends us to give is, "Nobody." It's the same as saying, "If God is for us, no one can be against us." That seems naïve. It's like saying when your head is cut off, "Not a hair of my head has perished." These excessive statements, it seems, are meant to say more than we have said so far. They intend to say something more than that dying saints won't be separated from Christ.

This "something more" comes out in the words "more than conquerors." "In all these things we are more than conquerors through him who loved us" (Rom. 8:37). What does "more than conquerors" mean? How can you be more than a conqueror when you risk for the cause of God and get hurt for it?

If you venture some act of obedience that magnifies the supreme value of Jesus Christ and get attacked by one of the enemies mentioned in verse 35, say, famine or sword, what must happen for you to be called simply "a conqueror"? Answer: you must not be separated from the love of Jesus Christ. The aim of the attacker is to destroy you, and cut you off from Christ, and bring you to final ruin without God. You are a conqueror if you defeat this aim and remain in the love of Christ. God has promised that this will happen. Trusting this, we risk.

But what must happen in this conflict with famine and sword if you are to be called *more* than a conqueror? One biblical answer is that a conqueror defeats his enemy, but one who is more than a conqueror subjugates his enemy. A conqueror nullifies the purpose of his enemy; one who is more than a conqueror makes the enemy serve his own purposes. A conqueror strikes down his foe; one who is more than a conqueror makes his foe his slave.

Practically what does this mean? Let's use Paul's own words in 2 Corinthians 4:17: "This slight momentary affliction is preparing [effecting, or working, or bringing about] for us an eternal weight of glory beyond all comparison." Here we could say that "affliction" is one of the attacking enemies. What has happened in Paul's conflict with it? It has certainly not separated him from the love of Christ. But even more, it has been taken captive, so to speak. It has been enslaved and made to serve Paul's everlasting joy. "Affliction," the former enemy, is now working for Paul. It is preparing for Paul "an eternal weight of glory." His enemy is now his slave. He has not only conquered his enemy. He has more than conquered him.

Affliction raised his sword to cut off the head of Paul's faith. But instead the hand of faith snatched the arm of affliction and forced it to cut off part of Paul's worldliness. Affliction is made the servant of godliness and humility and love. Satan meant it for evil, but God meant it for good. The enemy became Paul's slave and worked for him an even greater weight of glory than he would have ever had without the fight. In that way Paul—and every follower of Christ—is more than a conqueror.

THE ONLY ROAD THAT LEADS TO LASTING JOY

This is the promise that empowers us to take risks for the sake of Christ. It is not the impulse of heroism, or the lust for adventure, or the courage of self-reliance, or the need to earn God's favor. It is simple trust in Christ—that in him God will do everything necessary so that we can enjoy making much of him forever. Every good poised to bless us, and every evil arrayed against us, will in the end help us boast only in the cross, magnify Christ, and glorify our Creator. Faith in these promises frees us to risk and to find in our own experience that it is better to lose our life than to waste it.

Therefore, it is right to risk for the cause of Christ. It is right to engage the enemy and say, "May the Lord do what seems good to him." It is right to serve the people of God, and say, "If I perish, I perish!" It is right to stand before the fiery furnace of affliction and refuse to bow down to the gods of this world. At the end of every other road—secure and risk-free—we will put our face in our hands and say, "I've wasted it!" But at the end of the road of risk, taken in reliance on the blood-bought promises of God, there will be fullness of joy and pleasures forevermore.

⽸ desiringGod

If you would like to explore further the vision of God and life presented in this book, we at Desiring God would love to serve you. We have thousands of resources to help you grow in your passion for Jesus Christ and help you spread that passion to others. At our website, www.desiringGod.org, you'll find almost everything John Piper has written and preached, including more than forty books. We've made over thirty years of his sermons available free online for you to read, listen to, download, and in some cases watch.

In addition, you can access hundreds of articles, find out where John Piper is speaking, learn about our conferences, and browse our online store. John Piper receives no royalties from the books he writes and no compensation from Desiring God. The funds are all reinvested into our gospel-spreading efforts. Desiring God also has a whatever-you-can-afford policy, designed for individuals with limited discretionary funds. If you'd like more information about this policy, please contact us at the address or phone number below. We exist to help you treasure Jesus Christ and his gospel above all things because he is most glorified in you when you are most satisfied in him. Let us know how we can serve you!

Desiring God
Post Office Box 2901 Minneapolis, Minnesota 55402
888.346.4700   mail@desiringGod.org